SALEM WITCH TRIALS

A BRIEF HISTORY FROM BEGINNING TO END

HISTORY HUB

Bonus Downloads

*Get Free Books with **<u>Any Purchase</u>** History Shorts*

Every purchase comes with a FREE download!

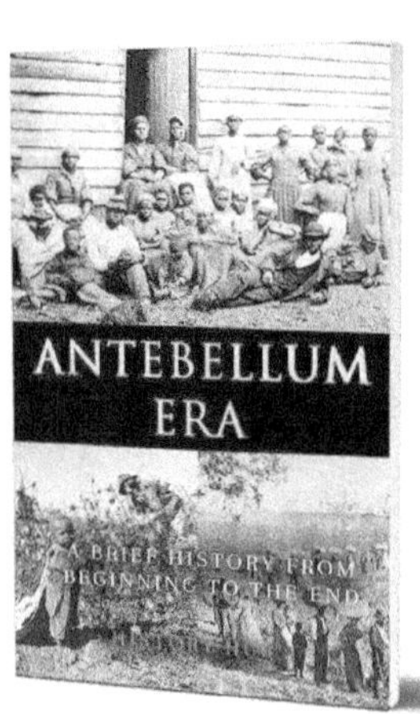 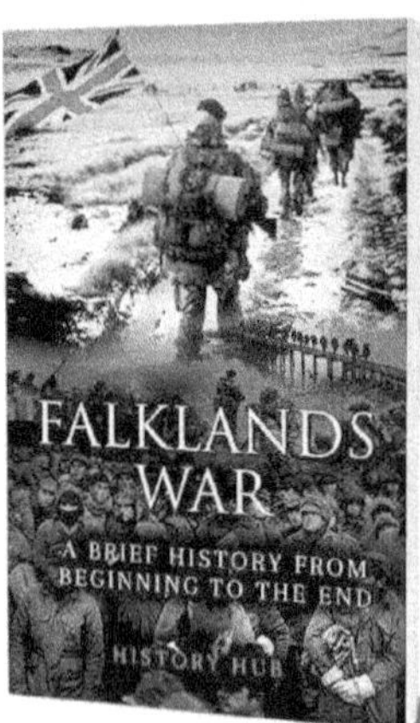 

Salem Witch Trials

A Brief History from Beginning to the End

History Shorts

© 2022 Copyright by History Shorts. All Rights Reserved.

Please Note: The book you are about to enjoy is an analytical review meant for educational and entertainment purposes as an unofficial companion. If you have not yet read the original work, please do before purchasing this copy.

Disclaimer & Terms of Use: No part of this publication may be reproduced or retransmitted, electronic or mechanical, without the written permission of the publisher. The information in this book is meant for educational and entertainment purposes only and the publisher and author make no representations or warranties with respect to the accuracy or completeness of these contents and disclaim all warranties such as warranties of fitness for a particular purpose. Product names, logos, brands, and other trademarks featured or referred to within this publication are the property of their respective trademark holders and are not affiliated with this publication. This is an unofficial summary and analytical review meant for educational and entertainment purposes only and has not been authorized, approved, licensed, or endorsed by the original book's author or publisher and any of their licensees or affiliates.

CONTENTS

Chapter One

Introduction

The Salem Witch Trials, made famous in *The Crucible* by Arthur Miller, still puzzle people today. It seems quite impossible that a few mischievous or hysterical children could cause the deaths of so many adults.

These trials occurred in colonial Massachusetts from 1692 to 1693. A period of mass hysteria caused more than 200 people to be accused of witchcraft and 20 to be horribly executed. The colony eventually recognized that the trials were unjust, which didn't help the victims even though compensation was paid to their families. To this day, the tale of the trials is synonymous with injustice and hysterical paranoia, and it still fascinates and intrigues popular imagination 300 years later.

In earlier centuries and even now, in certain parts of the world, like rural Africa, many Christians and people of different religions had a powerful belief that Satan or the Devil could give specific people known as witches the authority to hurt other people in return for their devotion, allegiance, and their souls. A "witchcraft obsession" was dominant throughout Europe, especially in the UK for three hundred years, from

1300 to 1700. Thousands of presumed witches, usually women, were often gruesomely killed after being tortured. The Salem trials happened as the European obsession with witches became less intense.

In 1689, English royalty King William and Queen Mary began a war against France in the American colonies known as King William's War. It devastated the regions of Nova Scotia, Quebec, and upstate New York, forcing refugees into Essex County and, mainly, into Salem Village in Massachusetts. (Salem Village is now called Danvers, Massachusetts, while the colonial Salem Town is now called Salem.)

The refugees created a burden on Salem's reserves and resources. This was exacerbated by the prevailing rivalry between the families linked to the prosperous port of Salem and those who were dependent on agriculture for their livelihood. There was also brewing controversy over the unpleasant Reverend Samuel Parris, Salem Village's first appointed pastor in 1689, who was generally loathed because of his stringent uncompromising manner and selfish nature. The Puritans thought all the arguing and quarrelsomeness was the Devil's work and disliked confrontational situations.

In January of 1692, the 9-year-old daughter of Reverend Parris, Elizabeth, and his 11-year-old niece Abigail Williams began having "fits." They shouted, hurled objects around, made bizarre sounds, and twisted themselves into unnatural positions. The local doctor was summoned, and he blamed their behavior on the supernatural. A local 12-year-old girl, Ann Putnam, suffered similar incidents. On 29 February, after being put under pressure by the magistrates Jonathan Corwin and John Hathorne, the girls accused three local women for their affliction. They blamed Tituba, Reverend Parris' Caribbean slave, Sarah Good, a beggar without a home, and Sarah Osborne, a poor older woman.

All three women were taken to the local magistrates on 1 March and cross-examined for some days. Osborne and Good asserted their innocence, but Tituba made the following alarming confession: "The Devil came to me and bid me serve him." She described in elaborate detail visitations by black dogs, red cats, and yellow birds, further claiming to have seen a "black man" who wished her to sign her name in his book. She acknowledged that she had signed this book and told the magistrates that there were several other witches in the town intent on destroying the Puritans. All three of the women were jailed after this confession.

Once the seeds of paranoia were planted, there was a flood of accusations over the next months. Charges were brought against Martha Corey, a devout member of the Puritan Church in Salem Village. This was of vast concern to the community. They felt that if Martha was believed to be a witch, then none of them were safe from being accused. The magistrates even interviewed Sarah Good's daughter Dorothy and took the four-year-old child's timid answers as a confession.

From April, Deputy Governor Thomas Danforth attended the hearings, and many more people from Salem and neighboring Massachusetts villages were interrogated.

On 27 May, Governor William Phips sanctioned the establishment of a Special Court. The first woman to be prosecuted by this court was a woman known to be a gossip and thought to be promiscuous. She was found guilty and, on June 10, was hanged on what came to be called "Gallows Hill."

Despite pleas from respected townspeople like Cotton Mather requesting that testimony based on dreams and visions be ignored, these were often used as evidence. Five people were hanged in July, another 5 in August, and 8 more in September. Governor Phips, as a reaction to Mather's petition and because his own wife was being investigated for witchcraft, forbade further detentions, freed many accused witches, and dissolved the Special Court on 29 October. Phips put a Superior Court of Judicature in place, and this court prohibited spectral information. As a result, only 3 out of 56 defendants were found guilty. Phips ultimately pardoned all imprisoned for witchcraft charges by the following May. The damage, however, could not be undone. Nineteen people were hanged, an eighty-year-old man was pressed with enormous stones until he died, and various people died in jail. Almost 200 people had been indicted for the practice of "the Devil's magic."

After the prosecutions and executions, many of those involved in the judgments, including Judge Samuel Sewall, publicly admitted to having made a mistake and being guilty of wrong judgment. In 1702, the sentences were called unlawful, and in 1711, the colony ratified a bill restoring the good names of those accused. They granted £600 in compensation to their heirs. However, it was only in 1957 that Massachusetts made a formal apology for the trials of 1692.

Let's have a closer look at what caused three children to bring chaos,

panic, and death to the village of Salem all those years ago.

Chapter Two
Witch Hunts

Before we examine the Salem trials, let's have a look at witch hunts throughout the world. These would have set the stage for the situation in Salem.

In Medieval Europe, witch hunting was a widespread phenomenon that reached its peak in the mid-17th century, just before the Salem trials. Witch hunters would go to incredible lengths to find and destroy witches. German inquisitor Heinrich Kramer even wrote a definitive book in 1846 about the recognition and treatment of witches.

Witches were identified by a sign on the skin, such as a birthmark or a mole. These were called the mark of the devil, and as most people have some form of blemish, this was an effective way to ensure they got all their target accused. It was also believed that a witch would have a companion, an evil spirit in the form of a domestic cat or dog.

Another way of proving guilt was pricking an accused with a pin. If they didn't bleed, it was a sure sign of being a witch. Some unethical witch hunters used retractable pins to ensure they got their prize.

Single older women without the protection of a man were highly suspect, especially if they had loose morals or were bad-tempered. People who used herbs for healing were also suspicious.

Having someone submerged in water to prove their guilt or innocence was also popular. An accused was thrown into deep water with a rope around their waist. If they floated, they were accused of witchcraft. If they sank, they would be declared innocent and pulled to safety. Unfortunately, many of them drowned during this process. In 1428, a systematic witch hunt was held in Valais. It lasted eight years, and 367 people were executed. In this case, mostly male peasants were condemned. They were arrested if three neighbors spoke against them. Their confessions of being able to fly or having been given power to injure others were extracted under torture. Their punishment was death by burning at the stake. As a merciful gesture, bags of gunpowder were tied around their necks to hasten their end. A famous person burnt for heresy and witchcraft was Joan of Arc. That was a political move, though, to get rid of her influence.

While burning was the execution method of choice in Europe, hanging was popular in England and America.

The biggest European witch hunt occurred in Bamberg, Germany between 1626 to 1631, where 900 people died at the stake. In 1626, the authorities were petitioned by local people asking why witches and wizards had caused frost to destroy their crops. An investigation found one woman guilty after confessing under torture. She also admitted to using Malevolent Magic, participating in a Witches Sabbath, and having sexual intercourse with Satan. The vast number of accused meant that a special witch house was built just to torture people by means of leg vises, thumbscrews, and strappado. Finally, the authorities were stopped by the emperor, but only after the Prince-Bishop had made a fortune confiscating the lands of the accused. The Prince-Bishop was replaced in 1631, ending the Bamberg witch trials. The last authorized witch trial occurred in Poland in 1775. The Doruchów witch trial apparently started after community members accused fourteen local women of using magic to hurt the wife of a local nobleman. Three of the women died during torture, and the remainder were burned at the stake. This witch trial was associated with the Polish parliament's 1776 prohibition of torture and witch trials.

There are various theories as to why the Europeans allowed such excessive witch hunting to happen. Like Salem, it had to do with political and economic instability, religious competition between Catholicism and Protestantism, and the Little Ice Age that caused general crop and livestock loss, resulting in disease and famine. These witch hunts were also fueled by selfish, greedy, and unethical witch hunters who made substantial amounts of money from uncovering and executing these so-called witches.

With increasing scientific knowledge and political and economic stability, the age of superstition passed into a more enlightened era, and witch hunting in Europe finally met its end after more than three hundred years. The last witch was executed in Europe only in 1782, and by this time, estimates have it that tens of thousands of people, mainly older women, lost their lives falsely accused as witches.

Witch hunting never really had much to do with witches. It had to do with greed, fear, superstition, and political and economic unrest, just as it did in Salem. The Salem witch trials and deaths arose as the result of a mixture of church politics, family quarrels, and bored, hysterical children, all of which happened in an environment without proper political authority.

Chapter Three
Salem The Background to the Trials

In the latter part of the 17th century, there were two towns of Salem. There was a busy, commercially viable port town on the Massachusetts Bay. This was known as Salem Town and would later develop into modern Salem. Approximately 10 miles inland from the port town was a small, poor agricultural population consisting of about 500 individuals known as Salem Village. The town had a marked social divide worsened by the unpleasant rivalry between the two dominant families: the wealthy porters connected with Salem Town's affluent merchants and the Putnam family who wanted greater independence for the village and supported and represented the less affluent farm families. Quarrels over property were common, and litigiousness was widespread.

In 1689, through the leverage of the Putnam family, Samuel Parris, a Boston merchant, became the minister of the town's Congregational church. Parris came via Barbados. Parris, who had studied theology at what is present-day Harvard University, had been unable to graduate but was, nonetheless, determined to change careers from being a businessman to being a minister. He brought his wife and three children, and his niece with him. He also brought his two slaves: John Indian and Tituba who were originally from Barbados. Historians aren't sure of their ethnicity, but they were possibly Caribbean or Indians.

Parris had carefully arranged a beneficial contract with his church elders, but fairly early in his term, he wanted a bigger remuneration, incorporating the title to the parsonage. This did not please members of the church community. Parris's traditional, rigid Puritan beliefs and preaching further split the congregation. This split was most apparent when he regularly asserted that people who were not congregation members should depart before holy communion. As a result, Salem split into factions that were either for or against Parris.

In 1692, the Salem witch trials were a dramatic occurrence that persisted for just over a year. With religious fervor inciting mass hysteria in the little colony, the Salem trials consisted of accusations and charges of witchcraft against many innocent people, and those who were unlucky would die. These prosecutions and the testimony related to them were based on the strict Puritan concept of good (God) versus evil (Satan). The Puritans were a group of people originally from England who escaped the fallout from the "Glorious Revolution" and made a home in Salem, Massachusetts. They arrived in America hopeful to start a new life that would be under the auspices of a new and uncorrupted church, as they thought the Church in England was full of corruption and deceit. They developed a "new" doctrine that was based on an amalgamation of Protestant and Catholic ideas and saw themselves as inspired by God. They had an uncompromising belief that all people needed to embrace their way of living to live devoutly and have a strong commitment to God. The Puritans founded these beliefs on the concept that achieving this pure life meant avoiding the temptations of the Devil.

When a series of unexplainable behavior among the young girls in the community occurred, the Puritans of Salem looked to their doctrine for explanations. The behavior went against their rigid belief system, and the only logical reason for this behavior was that God was angry and had allowed the Devil to bring disrepute and punishment into the community. In their effort to restore their bond with their God, they believed they had to rid their community of Satan and his minions. Satan was thought to have possessed the souls of some members of the community, and the

Puritans believed it was their God-ordained responsibility to be rid of them.

Because religion was the dominant force behind everything that happened in Salem, the belief that some people might have sold their souls to the Devil was not as strange as it would seem to us. The Puritans believed they were part of ongoing spiritual warfare. Their world was not just what they could see but what they perceived to be happening in the spiritual realm. Most of those accused were women. This was based on the Puritan belief that women were temptresses and inferior to men and thus susceptible to making wrong or misguided decisions.

This was the environment in which the hysteria and manipulation of the young girls found a fruitful response. Their behavior was like a spark to a powder keg that created an immediate terrified overreaction from the adults in the community.

Chapter Four
The Nature of Hysteria in Salem

Three hundred years after the Salem trials, there are still questions around the nature of mass hysteria that caused the disruption of a whole town and the execution of twenty innocent people.

What happened to cause those young girls to react as they did? The odds are good that it was a combination of factors that caused these young girls to throw themselves on the ground, writhe, cry out and twitch. The following reasons or a combination of them have been mooted for the behavior that sparked these dramatic events:

- There was a strong belief in the Puritan community that Satan was alive and well and trying to damage their health and community peace of mind. A range of common problems which we would explain by natural causes today were blamed on Satan. These include natural catastrophes, disease, and misfortune. The young, impressionable girls would have been very accustomed to hearing about the influence of Satan in the world.

- There was also a strong belief, based on previous witchcraft cases and a worldwide terror of witchcraft, that Satan would recruit witches, and occasionally wizards, to do his dirty work on earth.

- There was also a strong belief that witches would manifest specific symptoms, as described in the History of Witch Hunts. The girls would have known these symptoms, most of which could be faked.

- The people of Salem were going through a difficult time which would have made everybody wary that Satan was on the loose. There was smallpox in the town. The arrival of refugees meant that resources were strained, and people were experiencing poverty. They were also affected by frontier wars with Indians, which caused additional hardship.

- The fantastic stories of the slave woman Tituba would have stimulated the girls' imaginations, thus encouraging their strange behavior.

- Some historians have suggested that the children could have developed Convulsive Ergotism, which is a disease caused by eating infected rye. Most historians take this theory with a pinch of salt.

- The girls, being raised in a rigid Puritan household, were probably bored and wanted a little excitement. It's improbable that the whole affair was a prank. There was definitely hysteria involved, but it would have been difficult to admit wrongdoing once the process had begun.

- The magistrates and townsfolk were receptive to the idea of witches on the loose in Salem, so they would not look too closely at the evidence, particularly when they allowed spectral evidence. It also took the emphasis off their own wartime failures.

- Once witches, like Tituba, started to confess, they were vindicated, and the whole situation looked more credible.

- It was also the perfect stage to settle old disputes and grudges among the rival farming and harbor communities in Salem.

In a sense, all of these conspired to create a "perfect storm," which led to the circumstances that caused the Salem trials.

Other evidence has come to light in modern times of a disease called Mass Conversion Disorder. It's a psychogenic disorder that, while very rare, mainly manifests in young girls. It was originally named by Sigmund Freud as Mass Hysteria, and it manifests as extreme fear or anguish which causes physical symptoms. It's been described by experts as "motor-based hysteria." Although uncommon in the Western world, it's when long-term fear or stress causes disruptions to the brain which leads to physical symptoms like twitching, shaking, being in a trance state, and confused speech. The symptoms tend to disappear when the stress does, which happened in Salem when the Special Court was disbanded.

An infamous modern case of this disorder began with a group of high school girls in 2012 in the town of LeRoy. The girls had dramatic symptoms of twitching, tics, and muscle spasms. Most of the girls came from dysfunctional homes, which added to the peer pressure caused by being cheerleaders. The resulting furor added to their stress, as sports events were canceled, and they received significant news coverage. Modern motor-based cases are caused by restrictive environments and places of high stress. They are still quite common in rural Africa.

There's no concrete evidence to explain the behavior of the girls, which caused the trials. It seems likely, however, that a combination of the explanations listed above could have caused the type of Mass Hysteria that is now named motor-based hysteria, particularly when it manifests with strange physical symptoms. While the trials happened three hundred years ago, it's certainly led to a great deal of speculation among historians over the years.

When a series of unexplainable behavior among the young girls in the community occurred, the Puritans of Salem looked to their doctrine for explanations. The behavior went against their rigid belief system, and the only logical reason for this behavior was that God was angry and had allowed the Devil to bring disrepute and punishment into the community. In their effort to restore their bond with their God, they believed they had to rid their community of Satan and his minions.

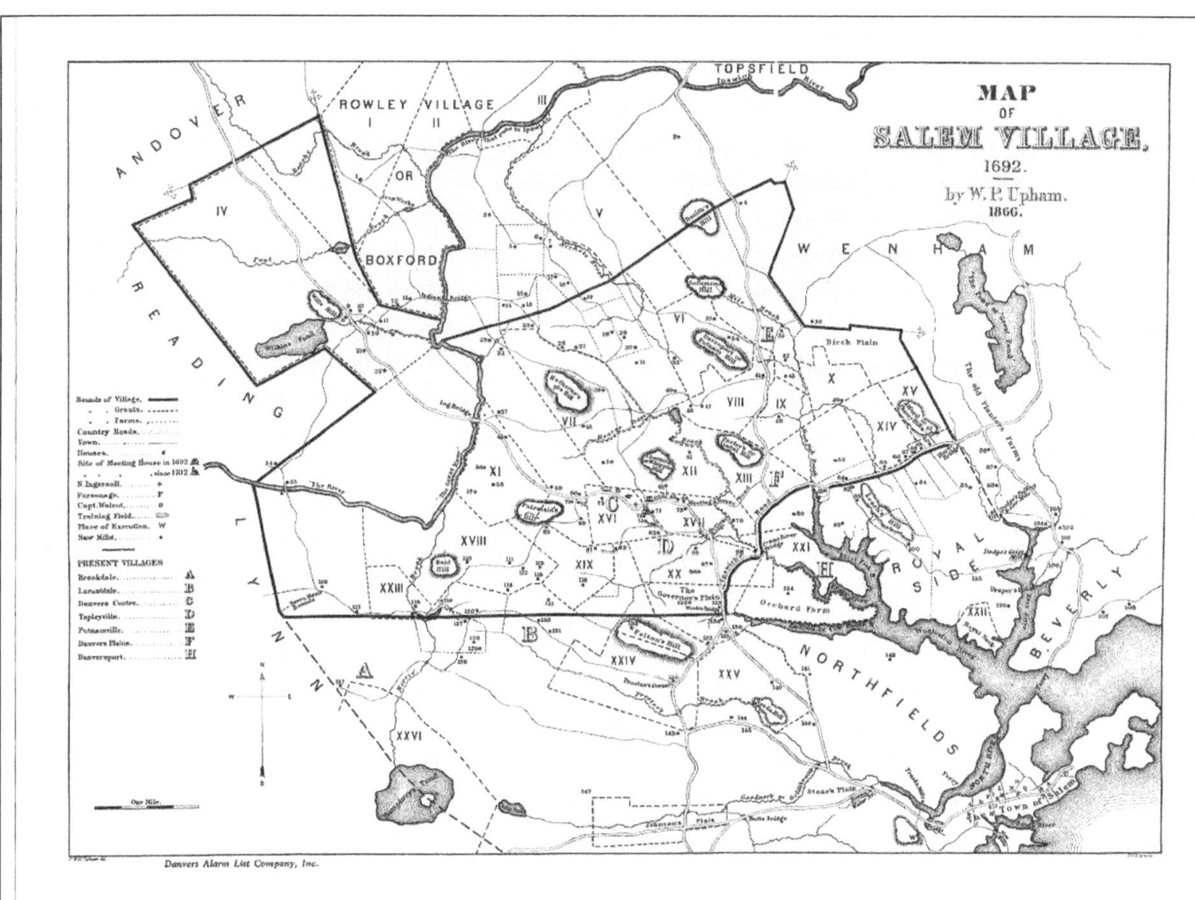

After the confession of Tituba, the magistrates decided that there must be evidence of the existence of other witches in the Salem community, and the unbridled hysteria increased. Possibly in an attempt to avoid being accused, young women placed themselves on the side of the accusers by joining in with the general hysteria. These other young women and girls started suffering fits, contortions and babbling, similar to those of the initial victims.

The above is a map of the town of Salem in 1692.

Chapter Five
Setting the Scene

Section 1. Fits and contortions

It is probable that the voodoo stories told by the slave Tituba stimulated the imaginations of three bored, strictly raised young girls. Nine-year-old Betty, Parris's daughter, his niece 11-year-old Abigail Williams and their 12-year-old friend Ann Putnam began by telling one another fortunes. This would be harmless enough behavior in another time or culture, but in rigid Puritan Salem, it created absolute chaos. Maybe the girls felt guilty for their behavior and decided to pass on the responsibility or perhaps hysteria caused their reactions, or they enjoyed the attention they received in a world where children were usually seen but not heard. Their behavior became increasingly eccentric, and irrational, throwing fits, screaming, and making strange sounds. They complained that they were being bitten and pinched, presumably by demons.

Section 2. Ergotism?

The strange behavior of the children has interested historians for years. It seems quite unbelievable that the eccentric behavior of hysterical children could have cost so much in human life and suffering, tear a community apart, and cause so much speculation for more than 300 years. Modern science has suggested some answers that have been examined by historians, but no definitive explanation has yet been accepted. Suggestions were made that the children might have had encephalitis, epilepsy or delusional psychosis, or even Ergotism, where the fungus that infects rye has an LSD-like effect and can create hallucinations and delusions. This would probably have been more feasible if just one child had been involved. Child abuse has also been punted. The Puritans were very authoritative, and the girls would undoubtedly have been beaten or spanked quite regularly as part of normal growing up in that community. Suggestions have been made that their reaction could have been a way to avoid punishment by turning the spotlight off themselves. Sexual abuse could also have triggered these excessive reactions. Some historians have studied the concept of "mythomania," where children lie by creating fantastic stories. Children nowadays are extolled as innocent of wrongdoing and incapable of harming anyone. They are seen as helpless and vulnerable. It is of interest, however, that children have been instrumental throughout history in causing witch hunts. Forensic experts have found that children, possibly to avoid punishment, make up lies but later come to believe them. Children are also very susceptible to suggestion, and a mischievous adult could easily set them off. No one knows what suggestions the slave woman Tituba might have made to the girls.

Children don't have a real grasp of consequences and might make up stories if they feel under pressure or if they think that these stories are expected from them. When they do create these stories, they might be motivated to achieve attention and to please adults or simply because they enjoy the power.

Section 3. The Witch Cake

The first attempt to point out those guilty of possessing the girls annoyed Parris enormously. A neighbor, Mary Sibley, suggested that a witch cake should be made with the urine of the three victims. Tituba made the cake which she fed to the dog. The dog was expected to manifest similar symptoms to the victims, but there is no record that it did. No results came from this strange experiment. Parris refused any more investigations like that, saying that it was blasphemous to use witchcraft to ferret out witches. Mary Sibley was banned from the church but later forgiven after a frank and full confession.

Chapter Six
The Young Witch Hunters

Section 1. Three witches

When Parris put pressure on the girls to name those who were tormenting them, Betty and Abigail claimed that Tituba and two other women had bewitched them. They chose two marginalized members of the community, and one must wonder who prompted their decision-making. Neither of the women accused were members of good standing in the community or a regular church attendee. Sarah Good was a bad-tempered beggar without a fixed abode, and Sarah Osborne was an old bed ridden woman who had an affair with a servant and was thus scorned by the community as a woman of loose morals. On 1 March, Jonathan Corwin and John Hathorne, magistrates from Salem Village, came to conduct an inquiry. Both women declared their innocence, although Sarah Good did accuse Sarah Osborne.

Section 2. Tituba

At first, Tituba professed to be innocent. Still, after being continually bullied (and unquestionably anxious because of her powerless slave status), she confessed to the two magistrates what they clearly wished to hear. She confessed that she had been called by Satan, who had visited her and forced her to make a pact with him. After three days of enthralling colorful testimony, she depicted meetings with the Devil's beast and with a tall, dark stranger from Boston who had summoned her to make her mark in Satan's book. She claimed to have seen the names of both Osborne and Good and the names of seven others that she was unable to read. She also confessed that Sarah Osborne owned a strange creature with two legs, wings and a woman's head. This weird confession convinced people that Satan was in their community.

Section 3. The Enigma of Tituba

What do we know about the slave Tituba, whose declarations in court provoked Salem's witch hunt?

Tituba's story is complicated and might be largely fictitious, but this is what history tells us: Tituba was a woman of color, probably native

American, who was a slave of Reverend Samuel Parris. Slavery from the colonies was rising, with many enslaved people coming from the West Indies. Tituba had been purchased by Parris in Barbados and had been a slave since childhood. She came to Massachusetts as a teenager and married another enslaved person called John Indian. They had a daughter named Violet.

Tituba looked after the Parris children. She no doubt regaled the children with stories of voodoo and overstimulated their imaginations. The girls were playing a game of fortune-telling involving pouring egg white into water. The egg white would form shapes that would help them read the future. When the egg white formed the shape of a coffin, the girls reacted by crying hysterically, barking like dogs, and babbling nonsense. This was in itself problematic because fortune telling was a grave sin in Puritan times. Tituba was not involved in fortune telling, but she baked the witch cake, which implicated her, and Parris beat her to get her to confess witchcraft as the reason for the girls' bizarre behavior.

Tituba confessed and enhanced her confession with an exaggerated story of how she had been instructed to serve Satan. She said that she rode on a stick with the children, and that a jet-black dog had commanded her to harm them. Tituba's statement was shocking and deeply disquieting to the good people of Salem. She had glimpsed "two rats, a red rat, and a black rat," she confided in the magistrates. Tituba admitted to pinching the two girls and informed the court about signing the "devil's book."

This was sufficient to incite hysteria in sleepy Salem. Tituba was officially accused of being a witch, and the other two women were indicted and charged with her. All three women were ideal targets for witchcraft accusations: poor, itinerant, and not respectable.

The community of Salem linked mysterious and supernatural practices like voodoo with people of color and Indians, and the townsfolk recognized Tituba as both. Her admission was sufficient to persuade the town that real evil was alive and well in Salem. As the prosecutions became more and more out of control, Tituba remained confined to jail in Boston. She was prosecuted as "a detestable Witch" and spent more than a year in jail.

Later, Tituba rejected her confession. She explained to the magistrate that she had devised the whole confession after Parris had beaten her. After the arrests were stopped, an anonymous benefactor paid her bail, and Tituba was freed. Tituba received no compensation, unlike the others accused of witchcraft.

In the period following the trials, Tituba became a popular figure in literature and folklore. Still, realistically, she was probably a minor figure whose low status in society left her in an ideal position to be a scapegoat in a town baying for blood.

Are You Enjoying Reading?

As an independent publisher

with a tiny marketing budget

we rely on readers, like you.

If you're receiving help from this book,

would you please take a moment to write a brief review?

We really appreciate it.

Chapter Seven
Five Notable Women Accused

Tituba's electrifying testimony sparked the famous witch hunt that had nearly 200 people prosecuted and 20 executed. Here are five of their stories.

Section 1. Bridget Bishop

In early June, when the Court of Oyer and Terminer was convened in Salem Town, its first case was against a local widow, Bridget Bishop. The prosecution expected her case to be an easy win as she had been accused of being a witch twelve years earlier. She also matched the conventional profile of a witch: old, impoverished, and aggressive.

Ten witnesses testified against Bishop, and she was convicted and condemned to death. On 10 June, she was "hanged by the neck until she was dead" at Gallows Hill.

Section 2. Sarah Good

By the time Bridget Bishop was executed, there were indications of resistance to the Salem Witch trials by various parties. Several pastors challenged the reliance of the court on spectral evidence. They fully believed that Satan could use people in his service, but they were not convinced of the existence of spectral figures tormenting the innocent.

Nonetheless, when the Court of Oyer and Terminer reopened their processes on 28 June after the successful conviction of Bishop, Sarah Good was rapidly condemned and sentenced to hang. Many afflicted women and girls alleged that Good's spirit or specter had assaulted them. Tituba and others had previously named her as a witch in their condemnations, asserting that she was seen flying on a broomstick and attending witches' gatherings. On 19 July, Good was transported by cart to Gallows Hill and hanged along with the respectable churchgoing Rebecca Nurse and three other women convicted as witches.

Section 3. Susannah Martin

Susannah "Goody" Martin was not even a resident of Salem but came from Amesbury, Massachusetts. Like Bishop, she had previously been indicted for witchcraft, but all charges had been thrown out for insufficient evidence. Her poor reputation probably spread to Salem because four of the possessed girls in Salem indicted her by name, alleging her specter had assaulted them.

When the court inquired how they realized the specter was that of Martin, the girls explained, "Oh, she said her name was Goody Martin, and she was from Amesbury." They did not actually have to see her. Despite the widespread absence of evidence against her, Goody Martin was condemned and hanged on 19 July with Sarah Good.

Section 4. Martha Carrier

When the controversial Court of Oyer and Terminer convened for its third session early in August 1692, it listened to the lawsuit against Martha Carrier of Andover. Andover would be home to many more implicated witches than any other town in the area. Her family was despised because they were believed to have carried smallpox to Andover. After Martha Carrier was indicted, the authorities examined her two sons, who were still teenagers, and tortured them into admitting to witchcraft and into accusing their mother.

When Cotton Mather wrote a book about the trials, he called Martha Carrier a "rampant hag" who desired to be "Queen of Hell." The court condemned Carrier at the same time as two well-known male scapegoats of the witch hunts. These men, John Proctor and Reverend George Burroughs were believed to be the ringleaders of Salem's coven. On 19 August, Martha Carrier was carted to Gallows Hill with Proctor and Burroughs and two other men. Unusually, no other women were hanged that day.

Section 5. Martha Corey

Martha Corey, like Rebecca Nurse, was not a conventional witch suspect, as they tended to be impoverished outcasts. She was a devout church member and was deemed to be an upstanding community member. Corey attracted some suspicion after she attempted to stop Giles, her husband, from going to one of the witch trials. She even tried to hide his saddle to prevent him. Soon after, an afflicted girl accused poor Martha of bewitching her and making her blind.

Martha's rebellious behavior turned the court officials against her. Giles declined to substantiate her testimony and actually testified against his wife. However, that attitude didn't last after he was accused himself. Less than a fortnight after Martha was convicted and sentenced to hang, Giles was pressed with heavy rocks until he died because he refused to implicate himself. On 22 September, Martha Corey was taken to the gallows with seven other alleged witches in what were to be the final hangings of the Salem Witch trials.

An illustration of Tituba by artist John W. Ehninger - The community of Salem linked mysterious and supernatural practices like voodoo with people of color and Indians, and the townsfolk recognized Tituba as both. Her admission was sufficient to persuade the town that real evil was alive and well in Salem. As the prosecutions became more and more out of control, Tituba remained confined to jail in Boston. She was prosecuted as "a detestable Witch" and spent more than a year in jail.

A painting of William Stoughton - Lieutenant Governor William Stoughton presided over the Court of Oyer and Terminer composed of seven judges. The accused witches were compelled to uphold their innocence without the assistance of legal counsel. What was most damning for these unfortunate accused was that "spectral evidence" was allowed as court evidence. Spectral evidence includes assertions by the accusers that they had recognized and been attacked by the spirits of the accused. In specter form, these witches had apparently bitten, punched, or contorted their victims. They claimed that Satan was using them to do his evil deeds. Even while the accused were testifying in front of the court, the young women and girls who were their accusers contorted, sobbed, and babbled in the Court Gallery. This was taken as evidence of the demonic presence within the accused.

Chapter Eight
Salem Witch Trials

Section 1. Salem Witch Trials

After the confession of Tituba, the magistrates decided that there must be evidence of the existence of other witches in the Salem community, and the unbridled hysteria increased. Possibly in an attempt to avoid being accused, young women placed themselves on the side of the accusers by joining in with the general hysteria. These other young women and girls started suffering fits, contortions and babbling, similar to those of the initial victims. These women and girls included Ann Putnam, Jr, and her mother. These were closely followed by Mary Walcott, Ann's cousin, and Mercy Lewis, the Putnams' servant. What was significant is that those they identified as witches were not just the marginalized and outcasts but were important community members. Notable among these was Rebecca Nurse, an older woman of some stature in the community. As time passed, many of those indicted were enemies of the Putnam family, and many of the accusers were from the Putnam family.

Section 2. The Court of Oyer and Terminer

On 27 May 1692, after some weeks of non-formal hearings and a spate of imprisonments, Governor Sir William Phips of the Massachusetts Bay Colony, intervened and authorized the convening of the official Court of Oyer, which means to hear and Terminer, which means to decide. Lieutenant Governor William Stoughton presided over this court composed of seven judges. The accused witches were compelled to uphold their innocence without the assistance of legal counsel. What was most damning for these unfortunate accused was that "spectral evidence" was allowed as court evidence. Spectral evidence includes assertions by the accusers that they had recognized and been attacked by the spirits of the accused. In specter form, these witches had apparently bitten, punched, or contorted their victims. They claimed that Satan was using them to do his evil deeds. Even while the accused were testifying in front of the court, the young women and girls who were their accusers contorted, sobbed, and babbled in the Court Gallery. This was taken as evidence of the demonic presence within the accused.

Section 3. The Confessions

Those accused who confessed to being witches and, more particularly, those who confessed and blamed other people for being witches were not punished by the court. Puritan beliefs meant that those who confessed would be given their retribution from God one day in the afterlife. Those accused who asserted their innocence were met with a harsh sentence, becoming victims and martyrs because they would not compromise themselves, knowing they were innocent. Many others in the community who knew that the unfolding incidents were travesties of justice said nothing, fearful that they would be penalized for putting forward criticisms of the court proceedings, and that they would be indicted for witchcraft. The situation in which the community found itself was one of fear and deep distrust. Neighbors were turning on their fellow neighbors, and even family members indicted one another. It was a terrible time to be alive.

Chapter Nine
The wages of Sin!

Section 1. The Convictions

On 2 June, Bridget Bishop was the first defendant to be condemned. On 10 June, she was hanged on what later would come to be called Gallows Hill. On 19 July, another five of the convicted were hanged. These included Nurse and Good. Good told the court that if she was a witch, the judge could be called a wizard. George Burroughs, a previous minister of Salem Village, was prosecuted for being the ringleader of the circle of witches. He, too, was sentenced and, with four others, was hanged on 19 August. Before he mounted the gallows, he spoke the Lord's Prayer without faltering. This was something that no witch was supposed to be able to do. This raised questions about his guilt for some of the attendees. Any objections were suppressed by Mather and others, and on 22 September, another eight convicted individuals were hanged. These included Martha Corey, whose eighty-year-old husband, Giles, who, after being denounced for witchcraft, had refused to admit guilt. He had been tortured with "peine forte et sure" and pressed under heavy stones until he succumbed to his injuries two days later, which was a cruel and harsh punishment.

Section 2. The Spread of the Contagion

As the prosecutions gained momentum, charges spread to people from nearby communities, like Malden, Beverly, Andover, Gloucester, Marblehead, Lynn, Boston, and Charlestown. On 3 October, the father of Cotton Mather, Increase Mather, who was an important minister and the influential president of Harvard, denounced spectral evidence and advised only taking into consideration direct accusations. He is famous for these words, "It were better that ten suspected witches should escape than that one innocent person should be condemned." The tide was turning against the witch hunters.

Section 3. Governor Phips

On 29 October, as the charges of witchcraft were broadened to include his wife, Governor Phips intervened, authorizing a stop to the legal proceedings of the Court of Oyer and Terminer. He appointed a Superior Court of Judicature and instructed it to disallow spectral evidence. When the trials began again, of the 56 people accused, three were sentenced, and even they, along with all those being held in jail, were pardoned by Phips. In May 1693, the trials ended. Nineteen people had been executed by hanging, and five others (excluding Giles Corey) had died in jail.

When the trials ended, they left behind a battered and bruised community. No one had been unaffected by the trials, and the deeply entrenched divisions in the community were further deepened by these events. It was a community with huge trust issues. Neighbors had turned on neighbors, and the church, normally an important and safe haven for Christian people worldwide, was uncomfortably shared by accusers and accused alike. The Salem community never really overcame these divisions, always being wary of one another. The trials also created a huge mistrust for the law and for authority figures, until the trials were finally found unlawful. Nonetheless, this was cold comfort for the families of those who had been unjustly executed.

Chapter Ten
The Aftermath and Legacy of the Salem Witch trials

Section 1. Aftermath

In the years following the trials, there were personal and institutional gestures of regret and repentance by various people and organizations involved in the Salem trials. In early 1697, the General Court of Massachusetts announced a day of contemplation and fasting for the hardships that had occurred due to the trials. In January 1697, one of the judges, Samuel Sewall, publicly admitted his own mistakes and remorse at the proceedings. The General Court in 1702 proclaimed that the trials were wrong and unlawful. In 1706, Ann Putnam asked forgiveness for her part as an accuser. Twenty-two of the thirty-three people who had been condemned were acquitted by the Commonwealth of Massachusetts in 1706. It also reimbursed £600 to the victims' families. The state of Massachusetts officially apologized for the Salem trials in 1957. It was only in 2001, however, that the final eleven of the convicted were completely vindicated.

Section 2. Literature: The Crucible

The Crucible, written by Arthur Miller in 1963, is a fictional representation of the Salem Witch trials. It looks at three main themes: the harm caused by lying, the importance of reputation, and the roles of corruption and mass hysteria.

- The destructive power of lying: Abigail and her companions told lies to evade being punished for rule-breaking. They were afraid of the consequences of their behavior, but these lies caused lives to be lost, human misery, and finally destroyed the Salem community.

- The significance of having a good reputation: As the prosecutions and indictments escalated, the townsfolk of Salem made emotional judgments founded on reputation. They accused marginalized people. They also fought to defend their own reputations. A perfect example of this is when Governor Phips abandoned the trials once his own wife was accused.

- The roles of hysteria and corruption: The play examines how during the Salem trials, mass hysteria enabled people's personal

intentions and motives to displace justice and logic. It also
examines the importance of not mindlessly following beliefs and
opinions imposed either by religion or by those in authority.

Section 3. The Symbolism

The Salem Witch trials and the subsequent witch hunt have become
symbols of the persecution of minorities. This symbolism continued into
the 20th and 21st centuries, largely because of Arthur Miller's
representation in The Crucible of the circumstances and people from 1692
as symbolic stand-ins for the anti-communist legal examinations by
Senator Joseph McCarthy during the "Red Scare" in the 1950s.

As the population of Salem lived in perpetual fear of being accused of
witchcraft, the people of the United States lived in fear of being ousted as
communists. Hollywood even blacklisted people who were indicted
during the McCarthy hearings. Miller had a personal experience of this
after a close friend of his accused seventeen people of being communists.
People who watched The Crucible immediately saw the comparisons
between the Salem Witch hunts and the McCarthy Witch hunts. Arthur
Miller had made his point.

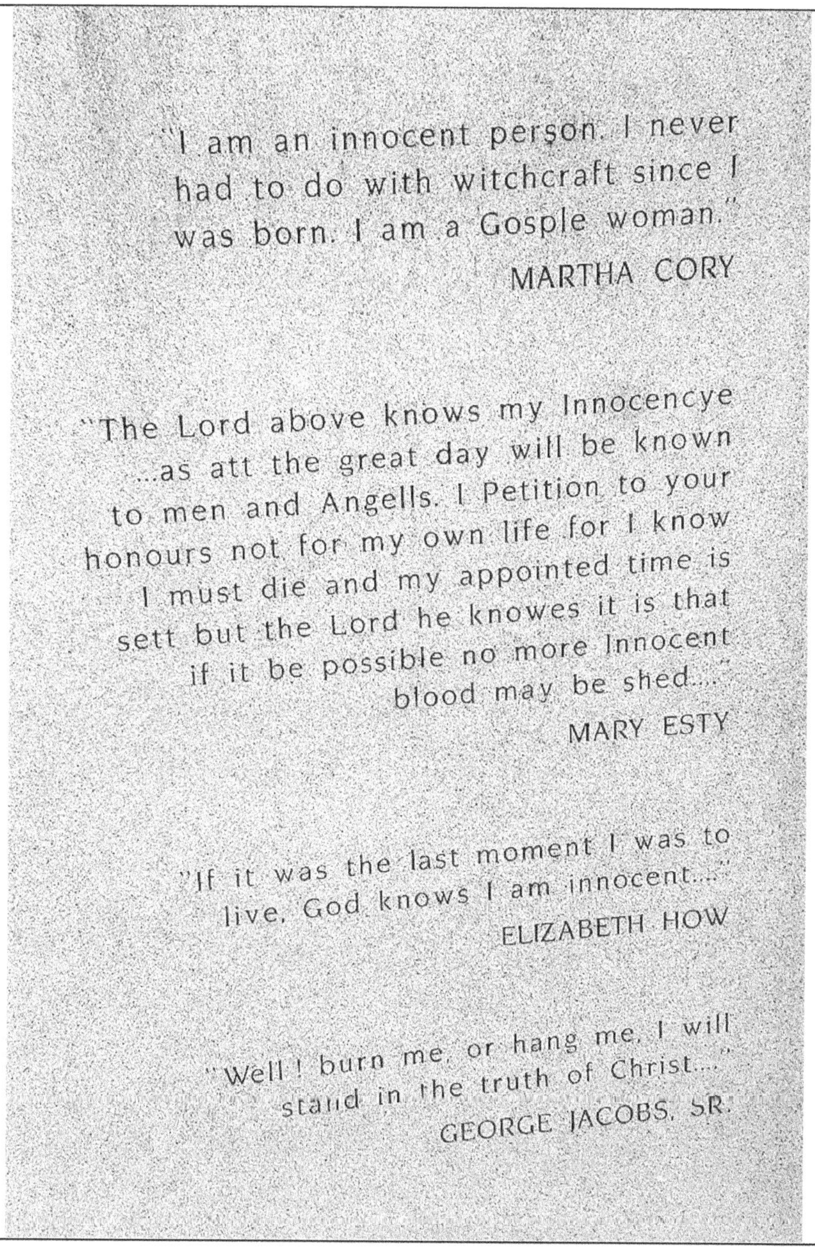

Featured above are the statements of the innocent. These statements form part of a memorial which was erected in Danvers, Massachusetts. These statements are a testament to the innocent lives lost during the Puritan purge of witches from Salem.

Abigail Williams testifyeth & saith that an old man that goes with two sticks hath appeared to & hurt her many times by pinching & bringing the book for her to set her hand unto, & the man told her his name was Jacobs the Father of Geo: Jacobs & the Grand-father of Margaret Jacobs & he had made said Margaret set her hand to the book & Sarah Churchwell & his son Geo: Jacobs & his wife & another woman & her husband viz: mr. English & his wife. also that the said Margaret had hurt her pretty much to day & at other times & brought her the book several times to night but not before.

We whose names are underwritten testifye that we heard the above sd Abigail relate the charge aforsd. this · 10· th May ·1692

Nathaniel Jngersoll

Jonathan Walcott

John Lorutt

Featured above is the deposition of Abigail Williams. In January of 1692, the 9-year-old daughter of Reverend Parris, Elizabeth, and his 11-year-old niece Abigail Williams began having "fits." They shouted, hurled objects around, made bizarre sounds, and twisted themselves into unnatural positions. The local doctor was summoned, and he blamed their behavior on the supernatural. A local 12-year girl, Ann Putnam, suffered similar incidents. On 29 February, after being put under pressure by the magistrates Jonathan Corwin and John Hathorne, the girls accused three local women for their affliction. They blamed Tituba, the Reverend Parris' Caribbean slave, Sarah Good, a beggar without a home, and Sarah Osborne, a poor older woman.

Chapter Eleven
The influence of the Salem Witch Trials on the American Justice System

The Salem witch trials would make a significant contribution to changes in court procedures in the US. They played a significant role at the beginning of the right to legal representation of any accused, whether they could afford it or not, the right to cross-examination of an accuser, and the presumption that an accused is innocent until proven guilty, which is a fundamental right underlying the justice system in the US today. During the Salem trials, an accused was assumed to be guilty. The presumption of innocence, which is the fundamental basis of a fair trial in modern times, was one of the main reasons why the Salem trials were so unjust.

Another thing lacking was the hearsay rule, a complicated legal doctrine that prevents the use of statements made outside of court at the trial. It ensures that admitted evidence is reliable and based on the personal knowledge of witnesses, not on what they heard was said at another time. It prevents assumptions and gossip from being mistaken for evidence.

Although the debate over allowing hearsay had already begun in the late 1600s, it was by no means applied at that stage.

A second major flaw in the Salem trials that has since been addressed is the right to legal representation of an accused. There was no requirement for defense lawyers or for cross-examination of witnesses before. If there had been, most witnesses could have been effectively challenged.

Another major legal flaw was the reliance on spectral evidence. It seems absurd to us, in the modern times, that a person could accuse someone else of being visited and threatened by a specter. This practice was dubious even during the times of the Salem trials. Cotton Mather warned against using spectral evidence, but the magistrates wanted a speedy resolution to the witchcraft curse, so it was disregarded.

Despite the minister's lukewarm opposition to spectral evidence, the Court of Oyer and Terminer proceeded to condemn indicted witches on spectral evidence. The situation was so bad in September 1692 that seven women and one man were executed as witches on one day. By then, though, public backing for the court was dwindling. Mather went public with his decisive resistance to using spectral evidence in the witchcraft trials, asserting in his book Cases of Conscience that it would be better for witches to escape detection than for an innocent person to die wrongfully.

The trials didn't stop because people no longer believed in witches. They stopped because people quit accepting that the trials were accomplishing a significant job at identifying witches. On 29 October 1692, Phips dissolved the Special Court, and by May 1693, Phips had acquitted and freed those still in prison for witchcraft. In future years, judges and magistrates asked forgiveness for their part in the trials. In 1711, Massachusetts ratified legislation exonerating those hanged as witches and compensating their families.

While it is difficult to make a direct assumption from the witch trials in Salem to current legal doctrine, there is no question they had an enormous influence on how people think about the law nowadays. The trials are crammed with cautionary anecdotes about how badly wrong things can go when legal processes neglect to offer minimum protection to the accused as well as accusers.

This bronze artwork stands in the center of Springfield, Massachusetts. It was done in the likeness of one of the founders of the town, Deacon Samuel Chapin. This piece is entitled "The Puritan" and gives an accurate account of how they would have looked and dressed. The artist of this piece remains unknown.

Chapter Twelve
Conclusion

The Salem trials teach us of the many flaws in the legal system, which have been addressed over the years so that people can have legal representation and are considered innocent until proven guilty. Still, the proceedings in Salem deliver many other important lessons. They substantiate the significance of impartial judges. They demonstrate the dangers of integrating church and state, and they underline the importance of a permanent judicial structure.

But Salem's most significant lessons go beyond the effects of legal systems and lawyers. The greatest dangers in Salem were not the prosecutors or judges. They were ignorance and fear. Ignorance includes: ignorance of science or history and ignorance of the disparity between the demons of our imaginations and real threats. Fear manifests as fear of things one does not understand; fear of the unknown; fear of people who are different from us and fear of telling the truth to powerful authorities or leaders.

The Salem trials prompt us to be careful of the problems that fear and ignorance create, even in our own time, in our own communities, and in our own minds and hearts. They beckon us to a position of reason, courage, and sound mind, and they alert us to what can transpire if we permit ourselves to be governed by our imaginations and fears.

If we can take positives from the Salem trials, it's that we have come a long way from being governed by fear of the occult and of being hanged at a whim by our disgruntled neighbors. Nonetheless, there are significant warnings to be taken from the trials. There are issues like judging people of different religions, color, gender, and culture. Religion, even nowadays, leads to extremism, terrorism, and wars. It reminds us that if we seek differences instead of similarities in the human race, we will invite, in some way or another, a negative reaction from other people.

The Salem trials were also about greed and competition in an economically challenging time. These are issues we all confront until today. Quite frankly, there are too many people on the planet, and resources are finite. The earth and the environment are under pressure, and economic wars and hardships abound.

Salem had a strong divide between the haves and the have-nots, which made their society unequal, with justice only for the rich. This is no different from our current situation in many parts of the world, where greed oppresses people and the rich nations and the rich within nations steal from those who cannot fight back.

Notwithstanding this, however, we are a lot better off in the modern world, particularly in first-world countries where social responsibility does work in favor of the citizens of the country. It's only in dictatorships and governments ruled by religious extremism that one could still be executed at a whim without a fair trial. It's up to us to ensure that we apply the lessons from the Salem trials to our own lives, communities, and countries so that fear and ignorance are not allowed to take hold, and in this way, we can make a difference.

Chapter Thirteen

Discussion Question

The Salem witch trials came at the end of a long period of European witch hunts. How did they differ from the American ones? Why do you think witch trials were so popular at this time?

Discussion Question

When *The Crucible* was written, it was as a direct dig at the McCarthy

witch hunts. What were they? Do you agree with the comparisons?

Discussion Question

The mass hysteria of the young girls is not that uncommon even

nowadays. Can you find other examples? Do you think that their

behavior was psychological? Justify your answer.

Discussion Question

How much of the witchcraft accusations were caused by fear, and how much by spite and jealousy? Why do you think as you do? Justify your answer.

Discussion Question

Why do you think Tituba told the lies she did? Was it fear or mischief?

What do you think?

Discussion Question

How did the legal system change because of the Salem trials? Do you think criminals are offered too much protection nowadays? What's your take on the subject?

Discussion Question

What do you understand by spectral evidence? Do you believe in its

legitimacy? Yes or no?

Discussion Question

"It was better that ten suspected witches should escape than that one innocent person should be condemned." Who said this? What was the implication of his words?

Discussion Question

What economic and social situations were affecting the town of Salem, which could have added the spark that started the witch hunts? List at least three. Elaborate on them.

Discussion Question

Could boredom and mischief have caused the children to accuse their

elders? Are children as innocent and vulnerable as we like to think they

are? What's your opinion?

Chapter Fourteen
Quiz Question

1. **True/False:** A strange disease infected the Salem witch accusers. This was caused by eating contaminated rye. The name of the illness is Ergotism.

2. **True/False:** Tituba was a witch who possessed the young girls. She practiced voodoo. She was an evil woman.

3. **True/False:** The Salem witch trials occurred in Massachusetts. They affected the town of Salem. They also spilled over into neighboring areas.

4. **True/False:** The Salem witches were punished by execution. This was normally done by being burnt at the stake. It was a cruel death.

5. **True/ False:** There was a real rivalry between the Harbor community and the agricultural community. The Harbor people were affluent. The agricultural community had been affected by an influx of settlers.

6. **True/False:** The first witches accused were poor and marginalized. They included the slave Tituba. They were unpopular members of society.

7. **True/False:** Governor Phips introduced the Special Court. He only did away with it when his daughter was accused of witchcraft. She was later hanged.

8. **True/ False:** Cotton Mather tried to caution the courts against allowing spectral evidence. He found it too difficult to believe, as indeed did most thinking people.

9. **True/ False:** Martha Corey was hanged as a witch. Her husband Giles was hanged alongside her. It was a terrible tragedy.

10. **True/ False:** F. Scott Fitzgerald wrote *The Crucible* in 1953. It was a play about the Salem Witch trials. It received high literary acclaim.

Quiz Answer

1. False: This is now considered to be very unlikely.

2. False: Tituba was a vulnerable slave woman who liked to tell stories to the young girls in her care.

3. True

4. False: They were executed by hanging.

5. True

6. True

7. False: It was his wife, and she was not convicted

8. True

9. False: He was pressed with heavy stones, and she was hanged

10. False: Arthur Miller wrote it.

Bibliography

- The Salem Witch Trials. Wikipedia. https://en.wikipedia.org/wiki/Salem_witch_trials#/media/File:Witchcraft_at_Salem_Village.jpg

- A Map of Salem in 1962. Wikipedia. https://en.wikipedia.org/wiki/Salem_witch_trials#/media/File:Salem_Village_-_map_of_-_Project_Gutenberg_eText_17845.jpg

- An illustration of Tituba. Wikipedia. https://en.wikipedia.org/wiki/Tituba#/media/File:Tituba-Longfellow-Corey_(cropped).jpg

- A painting of William Stoughton. Wikipedia. https://en.wikipedia.org/wiki/Salem_witch_trials#/media/File:WilliamStoughton.jpg

- Statements of Innocence. Wikipedia. https://en.wikipedia.org/wiki/Salem_witch_trials#/media/File:Danvers_victims_memorial,_quotations_from_victims.jpg

- The Deposition of Abigail Willams. Wikipedia.

  https://en.wikipedia.org/wiki/Salem_witch_trials#/media/File:Ab

  igail_Williams_vs._Geo_Jabobs.jpg

- The Puritan. Wikipedia.

  https://en.wikipedia.org/wiki/Salem_witch_trials#/media/File:Th

  e_Puritan_by_Augustus_Saint-Gaudens_-

  _Springfield,_Massachusetts_-_DSC02513.JPG

Bonus Downloads

*Get Free Books with **Any Purchase** History Shorts*

Every purchase comes with a FREE download!

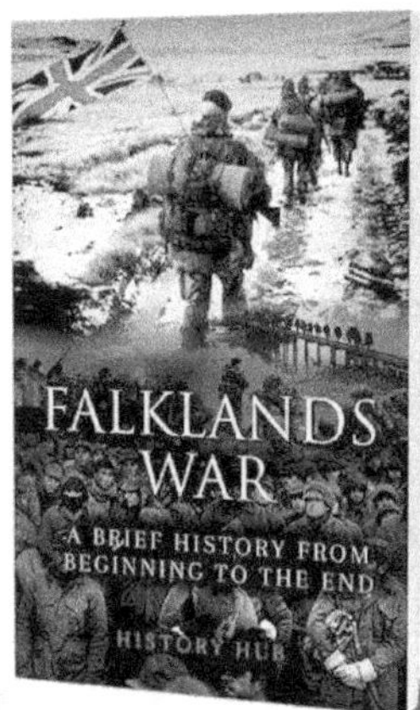

Thank You For Reading

As an independent publisher

with a tiny marketing budget

we rely on readers, like you.

If you're receiving help from this book,

would you please take a moment to write a brief review?

We really appreciate it.

www.ingramcontent.com/pod-product-compliance
Lightning Source LLC
Chambersburg PA
CBHW080612170726
48004CB00020B/1849